The *Essential* *Wit* of the
WORLD'S
FUNNIEST
PEOPLE

edited by
Daniel Bukszpan

FALL RIVER PRESS

New York

FALL RIVER PRESS

New York

An Imprint of Sterling Publishing Co., Inc.
1166 Avenue of the Americas
New York, NY 10036

ISBN 978-1-4351-6541-0

For information about custom editions, special sales, and premium and
corporate purchases, please contact Sterling Special Sales at 800-805-5489
or specialsales@sterlingpublishing.com.

Manufactured in the United States of America

2 4 6 8 10 9 7 5 3 1

www.sterlingpublishing.com

CONTENTS

✳   ✳   ✳   ✳   ✳

Introduction v

Kids Are People, Too 1

School Daze 8

The Aging Process 16

Doctor, Doctor 22

All You Need Is Love 29

Critters 37

In the Flesh 45

Money, Money, Money 52

The Battle of the Sexes 59

La Dolce Vita 66

Battle Royale 74

Jesus H. Christ! 79

Elected Office 85

The Fourth Estate 91

The Boob Tube 98

Fools 104

The Information Superhighway 110

Our Legal System 116

Showbiz 123

This Is the End 129

About the Editor 136

INTRODUCTION

Wit and comedy are often mistaken for each other, for the reason that the intended end result of both is laughter. The difference between the two is in the way each one gets there.

Wit often involves the use of wordplay and acute powers of observation. When it's successful, it's easy to imagine an enraptured audience of tuxedoed, mustachioed gents in monocles, sipping cocktails in some posh drinking establishment, and tittering politely at a droll comment about human folly—religion, politics, affairs of the heart.

Comedy, on the other hand, is what you get when someone on *America's Funniest Home Videos* gets beaned in the crotch with a football. You might still laugh, especially if there's no one around to see you, but it's really not the same thing. This is not to say that wit is at all times a more noble animal than broad humor. But anyone can elicit laughter by slipping on a banana peel, while a witty comment that hits its target is a little harder to get right.

In order for a comment to be witty, it should meet certain prerequisites. The saying that "brevity is the soul of wit" is absolutely true. Anybody hoping to be considered witty had better get to the point. The words should also have a brisk flow, with no commas, semicolons, or other exotic punctuation to gum up the works.

There are, of course, exceptions. A great many witty sayings have entered the general lexicon and stood for hundreds of years, all of which maybe run on a little too long or zig and zag when they could go in a straight line. These statements, for all their flaws, remain timelessly witty because they ring universally true to the eyes of the reader and the ears of the audience.

If the truth that it brushes up against is an uncomfortable one that people steer clear of in order to appear morally upstanding, even better. H. L. Mencken hit one out of the park with this quip: "Conscience is the inner voice that warns us that someone might be looking."

We all want to believe we're creatures of upstanding moral fiber and ironclad conscience. But the dirty, ugly fact is that we commit minor atrocities a hundred times a day, and it's only the judgment of others that stops us from taking that subway seat instead of offering it to the pregnant fellow commuter. If we thought we could get away with it, we would.

Mencken's comment shines a harsh fluorescent light on our contention that we are moral animals. No, we are not. We are selfish creatures whose initial and most powerful impulse is always "me first." We only ever behave commendably because the consequences of not doing so outweigh the desire to be seated during a twenty-minute subway ride. Phrasing it that way, however, would qualify as hectoring, and there's not much that's funny about that.

The art, the wit, is in saying it compactly, in language that gets us to quietly and privately incriminate ourselves. After all, having someone else call you out for your selfishness sucks. But if you can be set up to make the same observation about yourself, it can be a cleansing and pleasant experience, one that ultimately graduates to "truism" status as it gets repeated over the years. As of the time of this writing, Mencken has been dead for over sixty years, but nothing about what he said of our consciences needs to be altered one bit. It has remained timeless. It has remained true.

In compiling this book, it became necessary to cast about for people beyond the usual suspects—Mencken, Oscar Wilde, Mark Twain, Dorothy Parker, et al. However, certain people raised questions. For instance, George W. Bush has said some funny things, but we laugh *at* him, not *with* him. Disqualified.

There have also been some surprisingly amusing statements made by history's most abhorrent characters. But a quote by Josef Stalin, for example, would stop this book in its tracks, no matter how witty it might be. Disqualified.

After eliminating the ridiculous and the murderous, the quotes collected here came from a wide range of sources. Most of the quotes come from people with varied backgrounds, while many others are not exactly known as cut-ups. This is why you'll see George Carlin, Bill Murray, and Margaret Cho sharing space alongside Franz Kafka, Jean-Paul Sartre, and Werner Herzog. What they all had in common was the ability to quickly drill down to something truthful about mankind's folly in a matter of just a few words.

There are exceptions, of course, and some quotes go on for a little longer than others. The ability to elicit involuntary laughter was an essential piece of why the quotes were chosen, and so you'll see a few in this book that take anywhere from two sentences to a full paragraph to get to the point, simply because they passed the involuntary laughter test and were too good to leave out.

I'd like to thank Lindsay Herman and Chris Barsanti at Sterling Publishing for giving me the opportunity to compile this book. I'd also like to thank my parents, Albert and Joanna Bukszpan, and my sister, Claudia Bukszpan Rutherford, for their emotional support and encouragement.

Finally, I'd like to thank my wife, Asia, and my son, Roman. I love you both more than anything. You are my whole world, and I love going through life with you both.

—Daniel Bukszpan
December 2016

KIDS ARE PEOPLE, TOO

ing kids is part joy and part guerilla warfare.

—**Ed Asner**

The quickest way for a parent to get a child's attention
is to sit down and look comfortable.

—**Lane Olinghouse**

You can learn many things from children. How much
patience you have, for instance.

—**Franklin P. Adams**

We both liked children; we just didn't want any ourselves.
There were children everywhere, and we saw no reason
to start our own brand.

—**Thomas McGuane**

There are only two things a child will share willingly,
communicable diseases and his mother's age.

—**Benjamin Spock**

Grown-ups never understand anything by themselves,
and it is tiresome for children to be always and forever
explaining things to them.

—**Antoine de Saint-Exupéry**

Even when freshly washed and relieved of all obvious
confections, children tend to be sticky.

—**Fran Lebowitz**

Children are unpredictable. You never know what
inconsistency they're going to catch you in next.

—**Franklin P. Jones**

Cleaning your house while your kids are still growing is
like shoveling the sidewalk before it stops snowing.

—**Phyllis Diller**

How is it that little children are so intelligent and
men so stupid? It must be education that does it.

—**Alexandre Dumas**

*tting married and giving birth
...n that you have sold your life away
...ectly healthy people who can get their own
damn socks.

— Jennifer Crusie

I like children. If they're properly cooked.

—W. C. Fields

Before I got married I had six theories about raising children; now, I have six children and no theories.

—John Wilmot

We spend the first year of a child's life teaching it to walk and talk and the rest of its life to shut up and sit down. There's something wrong there.

—Neil deGrasse Tyson

Having a child is like getting a tattoo...on your face. You better be committed.

—Elizabeth Gilbert

Having children is like living in a frat house—
nobody sleeps, everything's broken, and there's a
lot of throwing up.

—**Ray Romano**

America used to live by the motto "Father Knows
Best." Now we're lucky if "Father Knows He Has
Children."

—**Stephen Colbert**

In America there are two classes of travel—first class,
and with children.

—**Robert Benchley**

The biggest thing I remember is that there was just
no transition. You hit the ground diapering.

—**Paul Reiser**

Sweater, n. Garment worn by child when its mother
is feeling chilly.

—**Ambrose Bierce**

We are accustomed to repeating the cliché, and to believing, that "our most precious resource is our children." But we have plenty of children to go around, God knows, and as with Doritos, we can always make more.

—Michael Chabon

My unhealthy affection for my second daughter has waned.
Now I despise all my seven children equally.

—Evelyn Waugh

A child is a curly, dimpled lunatic.

—Ralph Waldo Emerson

Every child that receives life advice should keep in
mind that in every parent's past, there's leftover booze
and contraceptives.

—Bauvard

SCHOOL DAZE

Education can get you the only thing that really matters in today's world—an assigned parking space.

— **Gene Perret**

Some students drink at the fountain of knowledge. Others just gargle.

— **E. C. McKenzie**

Remember in elementary school you were told that in case of fire you have to line up quietly in a single file from smallest to tallest? What is the logic in that? What, do tall people burn slower?

— **Warren Hutcherson**

The human brain is special. It starts working as soon as you get up and it doesn't stop until you get to school.

— **Milton Berle**

My education was dismal. I went to a series of schools for mentally disturbed teachers.

— **Woody Allen**

If there were no schools to take the children away from home part of the time, the insane asylums would be filled with mothers.

— **Edgar W. Howe**

In the first place, God made idiots. That was for practice. Then he made school boards.

— **Mark Twain**

I never did very well in math—I could never seem to persuade the teacher that I hadn't meant my answers literally.

— **Calvin Trillin**

As you can see, I have memorized this utterly useless fact long enough to pass a test question. I now intend to forget it forever. You've taught me nothing except how to cynically manipulate the system. Congratulations.

— **Bill Watterson**

A man who has never gone to school may steal from a freight car; but if he has a university education, he may steal the whole railroad.

— **Theodore Roosevelt**

My school was so tough, the school newspaper had an obituary section.

— **Norm Crosby**

I took a test in Existentialism. I left all the answers blank and got 100.

— **Woody Allen**

You know how to tell if the teacher is hung over? Movie Day.

— **Jay Mohr**

Education is learning what you didn't even know you didn't know.

— **Daniel J. Boorstin**

If you want to get laid, go to college. If you want an education, go to the library.

— **Frank Zappa**

In real life, I assure you, there is no such thing as algebra.

— **Fran Lebowitz**

Without a gentle contempt for education, no man's education is complete.

— **G. K. Chesterton**

Often, a school is your best bet—perhaps not for education but certainly for protection from an undead attack.

— **Max Brooks**

Thank goodness I was never sent to school; it would have rubbed off some of the originality.

— **Beatrix Potter**

There's always a bit of suspense about the particular way in which a given school year will get off to a bad start.

— **Frank Portman**

I won't say ours was a tough school, but we had our own coroner. We used to write essays like "What I'm Going to Be If I Grow Up."

— **Lenny Bruce**

Do you know the difference between education and experience? Education is when you read the fine print; experience is what you get when you don't.

— **Pete Seeger**

Education: the path from cocky ignorance to miserable uncertainty.

— **Mark Twain**

When asked "What do we need to learn this for?" any high-school teacher can confidently answer that, regardless of the subject, the knowledge will come in handy once the student hits middle age and starts working crossword puzzles in order to stave off the terrible loneliness.

— David Sedaris

I know the answer! The answer lies within the heart of all mankind! The answer is twelve? I think I'm in the wrong building.

— **Charles M. Schulz**

A woman with an education may be able to spend more time sitting in a chair instead of lying on her back.

— **Anne Bishop**

THE AGING PROCESS

The first sign of maturity is the discovery that the volume knob also turns to the left.

— Jerry M. Wright

You know your children are growing up when they stop asking you where they came from and refuse to tell you where they're going.

— P. J. O'Rourke

The maturing of a woman who has continued to grow is a beautiful thing to behold. Or, if your ad revenue or your seven-figure salary or your privileged sexual status depend on it, it is an operable condition.

— Naomi Wolf

The young always have the same problem—how to rebel and conform at the same time. They have now solved this by defying their parents and copying one another.

— Quentin Crisp

Growing up is losing some illusions, in order to acquire others.

— **Virginia Woolf**

I reckon responsible behavior is something to get when you grow older. Like varicose veins.

— **Terry Pratchett**

Don't try to make children grow up to be like you, or they may do it.

— **Russell Baker**

Growing up is such a barbarous business, full of inconvenience and pimples.

— **J. M. Barrie**

Parents often talk about the younger generation as if they didn't have anything to do with it.

— **Haim Ginott**

Middle age is having a choice between two temptations and choosing the one that'll get you home earlier.

— Dan Bennett

Life is a moderately good play with a badly written third act.

— Truman Capote

There is no pleasure worth forgoing just for an extra three years in the geriatric ward.

— John Mortimer

Age does not diminish the extreme disappointment of having a scoop of ice cream fall from the cone.

— Jim Fiebig

When you get to my age life seems little more than one long march to and from the lavatory.

— A. C. Benson

One of the delights known to age, and beyond the grasp of youth, is that of Not Going.

— **Anthony Burgess**

I've always dreamed of growing up to be Amy Poehler.

— **Amy Poehler**

Never tease an old dog; he might have one bite left.

— **Robert A. Heinlein**

Wisdom is the reward for surviving our own stupidity.

— **Brian Rathbone**

And meanwhile time goes about its immemorial work of making everyone look and feel like shit.

— **Martin Amis**

At 50, everyone has the face he deserves.

— **George Orwell**

It's paradoxical that the idea of living a long life appeals to everyone, but the idea of getting old doesn't appeal to anyone.

— Andy Rooney

If all women revealed their age, men would have nothing to hide from each other.

— Bauvard

The problem with aging is not that it's one damn thing after another—it's every damn thing, all at once, all the time.

— John Scalzi

DOCTOR, DOCTOR

Never go to a doctor whose office plants have died.

— **Erma Bombeck**

A Harvard Medical School study has determined that rectal thermometers are still the best way to tell a baby's temperature. Plus, it really teaches the baby who's boss.

— **Tina Fey**

You may not be able to read a doctor's handwriting and prescription, but you'll notice his bills are neatly typewritten.

— **Earl Wilson**

The great secret of doctors, known only to their wives, but still hidden from the public, is that most things get better by themselves; most things, in fact, are better in the morning.

— **Lewis Thomas**

In the name of Hippocrates, doctors have invented
the most exquisite form of torture ever known to
man: survival.

— **Edward Everett Hale**

You know what they call the fellow who finishes last
in his medical school graduating class? They call
him "Doctor."

— **Abe Lemons**

The art of medicine consists in amusing the patient
while nature cures the disease.

— **Voltaire**

I was going to have cosmetic surgery until I
noticed that the doctor's office was full of portraits
by Picasso.

— **Rita Rudner**

My health insurance is cheap, but there are trade-offs. When I wanted to get a colonoscopy they sent me a chimney sweep.

— **Greg Tamblyn**

A doctor can bury his mistakes, but an architect can only advise his clients to plant vines.

— **Frank Lloyd Wright**

My doctor told me to stop having intimate dinners for four. Unless there are three other people.

— **Orson Welles**

Though the doctors treated him, let his blood, and gave him medications to drink, he nevertheless recovered.

— **Leo Tolstoy**

If you're so pro-life, don't lock arms and block medical clinics, OK? Lock arms and block cemeteries.

— **Bill Hicks**

All sorts of computer errors are now turning up. You'd be surprised to know the number of doctors who claim they are treating pregnant men.

— **Isaac Asimov**

I become faint and nauseous during even very minor medical procedures, such as making an appointment by phone.

— **Dave Barry**

We approach people the same way we approach our cars. We take the poor kid to a doctor and ask, What's wrong with him, how much will it cost, and when can I pick him up?

— **James Hillman**

The most exquisite pleasure in the practice of medicine comes from nudging a layman in the direction of terror, then bringing him back to safety again.

— **Kurt Vonnegut**

Doctors always think anybody doing something they aren't is a quack; also they think all patients are idiots.

— **Flannery O'Connor**

You need a good bedside manner with doctors or you will get nowhere.

— **William S. Burroughs**

Sometimes, the only difference between a superhero and a supervillain is a malpractice suit.

— **Corey Redekop**

One of the most common and most dangerous misbeliefs is that it is impossible for someone to be stupid just because they are a doctor or a lawyer.

— **Mokokoma Mokhonoana**

Surgeons know nothing but do everything. Internists know everything but do nothing. Pathologists know everything and do everything but too late.

— **Robin Cook**

Doctors don't seem to realize that most of us are perfectly content not having to visualize ourselves as animated bags of skin filled with obscene glop.

— **Joe Haldeman**

ALL YOU NEED IS LOVE

Love is an exploding cigar we willingly smoke.

— **Lynda Barry**

Before you marry a person, you should first make them use a computer with slow Internet service to see who they really are.

— **Will Ferrell**

Real love amounts to withholding the truth, even when you're offered the perfect opportunity to hurt someone's feelings.

— **David Sedaris**

I love being married. It's so great to find one special person you want to annoy for the rest of your life.

— **Rita Rudner**

Marriage has no guarantees. If that's what you're looking for, go live with a car battery.

— **Erma Bombeck**

Love is a fire. But whether it is going to warm your hearth or burn down your house, you can never tell.

— Joan Crawford

First love is a kind of vaccination which saves man from catching the complaint the second time.

— Honoré de Balzac

Love is like an hourglass, with the heart filling up as the brain empties.

— Jules Renard

A youth with his first cigar makes himself sick. A youth with his first girl makes everybody sick.

— Mary Wilson

I love you no matter what you do, but do you have to do so much of it?

— Jean Illsley Clarke

It is easier to love humanity as a whole than to love one's neighbor.

— Eric Hoffer

What's the difference between a boyfriend and a husband? About 30 pounds.

— Cindy Garner

True love comes quietly, without banners or flashing lights. If you hear bells, get your ears checked.

— Erich Segal

Love is being stupid together.

— Paul Valery

Trust me, my parents have about as much impulse control as I do. If they didn't like you, you'd know. Hell, you'd have been sitting in the car until I finished eating.

— Billy London

Obviously, if I was serious about having a relationship
with someone long-term, the last people I would introduce
him to would be my family.

— Chelsea Handler

Love, I've come to understand, is more than three words
mumbled before bedtime.

— Nicholas Sparks

Love is only a dirty trick played on us to achieve
continuation of the species.

— W. Somerset Maugham

If loving someone is putting them in a straitjacket and
kicking them down a flight of stairs, then yes, I have
loved a few people.

— Jarod Kintz

The one who loves least controls the relationship.

— Robert Newton Anthony

It's no good pretending that any relationship has a future if your record collections disagree violently or if your favorite films wouldn't even speak to each other if they met at a party.

— **Nick Hornby**

Instead of getting married again, I'm going to find a woman I don't like and just give her a house.

— **Lewis Grizzard**

The difference between sex and love is that sex relieves tension and love causes it.

— **Woody Allen**

Love is much nicer to be in than an automobile accident, a tight girdle, a higher tax bracket or a holding pattern over Philadelphia.

— **Judith Viorst**

Marriage is like vitamins: We supplement each other's minimum daily requirements.

— **Kathy Mohnke**

What is irritating about love is that it is a crime that requires an accomplice.

— **Charles Baudelaire**

We are all mortal until the first kiss and the second glass of wine.

— **Eduardo Galeano**

True love is singing karaoke "Under Pressure" and letting the other person sing the Freddie Mercury part.

— **Mindy Kaling**

If I love you, what business is it of yours?

— **Goethe**

Love is a grave mental disease.

— **Plato**

CRITTERS

I love things made out of animals. It's just so funny to think of someone saying, "I need a letter opener. I guess I'll have to kill a deer."

— David Sedaris

God loved the birds and invented trees. Man loved the birds and invented cages.

— Jacques Deval

I ask people why they have deer heads on their walls. They always say because it's such a beautiful animal. There you go. I think my mother is attractive, but I have photographs of her.

— Ellen DeGeneres

At the zoo, all the animals have a decent composure, except for the monkeys. You get the feeling man is very close to them.

— Emil Cioran

Dogs feel very strongly that they should always go
with you in the car, in case the need should arise
for them to bark violently at nothing, right in
your ear.

— **Dave Barry**

If you hold a cat by the tail, you learn things you
cannot learn any other way.

— **Mark Twain**

New Rule: Stop leaving couches on the sidewalk.
Besides being lazy and ugly, it's animal cruelty. You
teach your dog not to pee on the couch, and then
when you take him to the place he's supposed to pee,
there's a couch.

— **Bill Maher**

Women and cats will do as they please, and men and
dogs should relax and get used to the idea.

— **Robert A. Heinlein**

People who keep dogs are cowards who haven't got the guts to bite people themselves.

— **August Strindberg**

Dogs will give you unconditional love until the day they die. Cats will make you pay for every mistake you've ever made since the day you were born.

— **Oliver Gaspirtz**

In ancient times cats were worshipped as gods; they have not forgotten this.

— **Terry Pratchett**

Cats have a scam going—you buy the food, they eat the food, they go away; that's the deal.

— **Eddie Izzard**

A dog teaches a boy fidelity, perseverance, and to turn around three times before lying down.

— **Robert Benchley**

We send one species to the butcher and give our love and kindness to another apparently for no reason other than because it's the way things are.

— **Melanie Joy**

We are obviously fascinated by the notion that dogs— or at least certain breeds of dog—might, just might, be really, really smart. It all makes as much sense as evaluating humans on our ability to sniff for bombs or echo-locate.

— **Jean Donaldson**

I am not a vegetarian because I love animals; I am a vegetarian because I hate plants.

— **A. Whitney Brown**

Cats are intended to teach us that not everything in nature has a function.

— **Garrison Keillor**

The better I get to know men, the more I find myself loving dogs.

— **Charles de Gaulle**

My favorite animal is steak.

— **Fran Lebowitz**

I would like to see anyone, prophet, king or God, convince a thousand cats to do the same thing at the same time.

— **Neil Gaiman**

Sometimes losing a pet is more painful than losing a human because in the case of the pet, you were not pretending to love it.

— **Amy Sedaris**

Cats are the lap-dancers of the animal world. Soon as you stop shelling out, they move on, find another lap.

— **Andrew Vachss**

Ｎew Rule: If you're one of the one-in-three married women who say your pet is a better listener than your husband, you talk too much. And I have some bad news for you: Your dog's not listening, either; he's waiting for food to fall out of your mouth.

— Bill Maher

Armadillos make affectionate pets, if you need affection that much.

— **Will Cuppy**

To my mind, the only possible pet is a cow. Cows love you … They will listen to your problems and never ask a thing in return. They will be your friends forever. And when you get tired of them, you can kill and eat them.

— **Bill Bryson**

IN THE FLESH

Sex is like air; it's not important unless you aren't getting any.

— John Callahan

We have reason to believe that man first walked upright to free his hands for masturbation.

— Lily Tomlin

Everything in the world is about sex except sex. Sex is about power.

— Oscar Wilde

Women fake orgasms and men fake finances.

— Suze Orman

Sex without love is a meaningless experience, but as far as meaningless experiences go, it's pretty damn good.

— Woody Allen

But when a woman decides to sleep with a man,
there is no wall she will not scale, no fortress she
will not destroy, no moral consideration she will
not ignore at its very root.

— **Gabriel García Márquez**

The main reason Santa is so jolly is because he knows
where all the bad girls live.

— **George Carlin**

What holds the world together, as I have learned from
bitter experience, is sexual intercourse.

— **Henry Miller**

I'm as pure as the driven slush.

— **Tallulah Bankhead**

Anyone who calls it "sexual intercourse" can't possibly be interested in actually doing it. You might as well announce you're ready for lunch by proclaiming, "I'd like to do some masticating and enzyme secreting."

— Allan Sherman

Geniuses and supergeniuses always make their own rules about sex as on everything else; they do not accept the monkey customs of their lessers.

— **Robert A. Heinlein**

It's not true that I had nothing on. I had the radio on.

— **Marilyn Monroe**

Sex at age 90 is like trying to shoot pool with a rope.

— **George Burns**

Sex and excretion are reminders that anyone's claim to round-the-clock dignity is tenuous. The so-called rational animal has a desperate drive to pair up and moan and writhe.

— **Steven Pinker**

Sex is kicking death in the ass while singing.

— **Charles Bukowski**

Dancing is a perpendicular expression of a horizontal desire.

— **George Bernard Shaw**

I have no objection to anyone's sex life as long as they don't practice it in the street and frighten the horses.

— **Oscar Wilde**

Sex should be friendly. Otherwise stick to mechanical toys; it's more sanitary.

— **Robert A. Heinlein**

Never play cards with a man named Doc. Never eat at a place called Mom's. Never sleep with a woman whose troubles are worse than your own.

— **Nelson Algren**

Anybody who believes that the way to a man's heart is through his stomach flunked geography.

— **Robert Byrne**

Sex is good, but not as good as fresh sweet corn.

— **Garrison Keillor**

A man in the house is worth two in the street.

— **Mae West**

How did sex come to be thought of as dirty in the first place? God must have been a Republican.

— **Will Durst**

MONEY, MONEY, MONEY

Money, Money, Money

It's income tax time again, Americans: time to gather up those receipts, get out those tax forms, sharpen up that pencil, and stab yourself in the aorta.

— **Dave Barry**

We Slovenians are even better misers than you Scottish. You know how Scotland began? One of us Slovenians was spending too much money, so we put him on a boat and he landed in Scotland.

— **Slavoj Žižek**

I made my money the old-fashioned way. I was very nice to a wealthy relative right before he died.

— **Malcolm Forbes**

Someday I want to be rich. Some people get so rich they lose all respect for humanity. That's how rich I want to be.

— **Rita Rudner**

The four most expensive words in the English language are "this time it's different."

— Sir John Templeton

It is better to have a permanent income than to be fascinating.

— Oscar Wilde

I love money. I love everything about it. I bought some pretty good stuff. Got me a $300 pair of socks. Got a fur sink. An electric dog polisher. A gasoline powered turtleneck sweater. And, of course, I bought some dumb stuff, too.

— Steve Martin

Money is better than poverty, if only for financial reasons.

— Woody Allen

I been shaking two nickels together for a month, trying to get them to mate.

— Raymond Chandler

If you think nobody cares if you're alive, try missing a couple of car payments.

— **Earl Wilson**

What is the difference between a taxidermist and a tax collector? The taxidermist takes only your skin.

— **Mark Twain**

The best way to teach your kids about taxes is by eating 30 percent of their ice cream.

— **Bill Murray**

Money, if it does not bring you happiness, will at least help you be miserable in comfort.

— **Helen Gurley Brown**

Anyone who lives within their means suffers from a lack of imagination.

— **Oscar Wilde**

If there is anyone to whom I owe money, I'm prepared to forget it if they are.

— **Errol Flynn**

Inflation is when you pay fifteen dollars for the ten-dollar haircut you used to get for five dollars when you had hair.

— **Sam Ewing**

Business is the art of extracting money from another man's pocket without resorting to violence.

— **Max Amsterdam**

I don't like money, actually, but it quiets my nerves.

— **Joe Louis**

People are living longer than ever before, a phenomenon undoubtedly made necessary by the thirty-year mortgage.

— **Doug Larson**

When you need to borrow money, the Mob seems like a better deal, I think. "You don't pay me back I break both yer legs." Is that all? You won't take my house or wreck my credit rating? Fine, where do I sign. Legs? Fine. You don't even have to sign anything.

— Craig Ferguson

The only reason I made a commercial for American Express was to pay for my American Express bill.

— **Peter Ustinov**

Money is something you have to make in case you don't die.

— **Max Asnas**

A bargain is something you can't use at a price you can't resist.

— **Franklin Jones**

Bills travel through the mail at twice the speed of checks.

— **Steven Wright**

THE BATTLE OF THE SEXES

In politics, if you want anything said, ask a man. If you want anything done, ask a woman.

— **Margaret Thatcher**

A gentleman is simply a patient wolf.

— **Lana Turner**

Most books on witchcraft will tell you that witches work naked. This is because most books on witchcraft were written by men.

— **Neil Gaiman and Terry Pratchet**

Woman is the dominant sex. Men have to do all sorts of stuff to prove that they are worthy of woman's attention.

— **Camille Paglia**

Can officially confirm that the way to a man's heart these days is not through beauty, food, sex, or alluringness of character, but merely the ability to seem not very interested in him.

— **Helen Fielding**

Behind every successful man is a surprised woman.

— **Maryon Pearson**

Watches are the only jewelry men can wear, unless you're Mr. T.

— **Gordon Bethune**

Here's all you have to know about men and women: women are crazy, men are stupid. And the main reason women are crazy is that men are stupid.

— **George Carlin**

God gave men a brain and a penis, and only enough blood to run one at a time.

— **Robin Williams**

Sometimes I wonder if men and women really suit each other. Perhaps they should live next door and just visit now and then.

— **Katharine Hepburn**

I require three things in a man: he must be handsome, ruthless, and stupid.

— **Dorothy Parker**

A woman's guess is much more accurate than a man's certainty.

— **Rudyard Kipling**

It is a well-documented fact that guys will not ask for directions. This is a biological thing. This is why it takes several million sperm cells ... to locate a female egg, despite the fact that the egg is, relative to them, the size of Wisconsin.

— **Dave Barry**

[Men] would rather lose an arm out a city bus window than tell you simply, "You're not the one." We are quite sure you will kill us or yourself or both—or even worse, cry and yell at us.

— **Greg Behrendt**

Never marry a man you wouldn't want to be divorced from.

— **Nora Ephron**

There are only three things women need in life: food, water, and compliments.

— **Chris Rock**

If we take matrimony at its lowest, we regard it as a sort of friendship recognized by the police.

— **Robert Louis Stevenson**

The basic conflict between men and women, sexually, is that men are like firemen. To men, sex is an emergency, and no matter what we're doing we can be ready in two minutes. Women, on the other hand, are like fire. They're very exciting, but the conditions have to be exactly right for it to occur.

— **Jerry Seinfeld**

Most women set out to try to change a man, and when they have changed him they do not like him.

— **Marlene Dietrich**

Women are cursed, and men are the proof.

— **Roseanne Barr**

At the age of eleven or thereabouts women acquire a poise and an ability to handle difficult situations which a man, if he is lucky, manages to achieve somewhere in the later seventies.

— **P. G. Wodehouse**

My wife and I were happy for twenty years—then we met.

— **Rodney Dangerfield**

Being a woman is a terribly difficult task since it consists principally in dealing with men.

— **Joseph Conrad**

To judge from the covers of countless women's magazines, the two topics most interesting to women are (1) Why men are all disgusting pigs, and (2) How to attract men.

— **Dave Barry**

A diplomat is a man who always remembers a woman's birthday but never remembers her age.

— **Robert Frost**

LA DOLCE VITA

I eventually decided that the reason Dr. Stone had
told me I was hypomanic was that he wanted to put
me on medication instead of actually treating me.
So I did the only rational thing I could do in the
face of such an insult—I stopped talking to Stone,
flew back to New York, and married Paul Simon a
week later.

— Carrie Fisher

Always do sober what you said you'd do drunk. That
will teach you to keep your mouth shut.

— Ernest Hemingway

Cocaine is God's way of telling you you are making too
much money.

— Robin Williams

A drug is not bad. A drug is a chemical compound.
The problem comes in when people who take drugs
treat them like a license to behave like an asshole.

— Frank Zappa

I hate to advocate drugs, alcohol, violence, or insanity to anyone, but they've always worked for me.

— **Hunter S. Thompson**

Even as a junkie I stayed true [to vegetarianism]—"I shall have heroin, but I shan't have a hamburger."

— **Russell Brand**

Let me be clear about this: I don't have a drug problem. I have a police problem.

— **Keith Richards**

After a few months in my parents' basement, I took an apartment near the state university, where I discovered both crystal methamphetamine and conceptual art. Either one of these things are dangerous, but in combination they have the potential to destroy entire civilizations.

— **David Sedaris**

I don't do drugs. I am drugs.

— **Salvador Dalí**

You know you're an alcoholic when you misplace things … like a decade.

— **Paul Williams**

If God dropped acid, would he see people?

— **Steven Wright**

Alcohol and marijuana, if used in moderation, plus loud, usually low-class music, make stress and boredom infinitely more bearable.

— **Kurt Vonnegut**

The worst gift I was given is when I got out of rehab that Christmas; a bottle of wine. It was delicious.

— **Craig Ferguson**

I used to have a drug problem, now I make enough money.

— **David Lee Roth**

Some contemptible scoundrel stole the cork from my lunch.

— **W. C. Fields**

I drink too much. The last time I gave a urine sample it had an olive in it.

— **Rodney Dangerfield**

A miracle drug is any drug that will do what the label says it will do.

— **Eric Hodgins**

Don't do drugs because if you do drugs you'll go to prison, and drugs are really expensive in prison.

— **John Hardwick**

It would be wryly interesting if in human history the cultivation of marijuana led generally to the invention of agriculture, and thereby to civilization.

— **Carl Sagan**

Of course I know how to roll a joint.

— Martha Stewart

Write drunk, edit sober.

— Ernest Hemingway

A meal without wine is like a day without sunshine, except that on a day without sunshine you can still get drunk.

— Lee Entrekin

I think pot should be legal. I don't smoke it, but I like the smell of it.

— Andy Warhol

I envy people who drink. At least they have something to blame everything on.

— Oscar Levant

The best pitch I ever heard about cocaine was back in the early eighties when a street dealer followed me down the sidewalk going, "I got some great blow, man. I got the stuff that killed Belushi."

— Denis Leary

An alcoholic is someone you don't like who drinks as much as you do.

— Dylan Thomas

Every loaf of bread is a tragic story of grains that could have become beer, but didn't.

— Walter Thornburgh

My father warned me about men and booze ... but he never said anything about women and cocaine.

— Tallulah Bankhead

Early to rise and early to bed makes a male healthy, wealthy and dead.

— James Thurber

BATTLE
ROYALE

Fighting for peace is like screwing for virginity.

— George Carlin

A conservative is a man who is too cowardly to fight and too fat to run.

— Elbert Hubbard

Never pick a fight with an ugly person. They've got nothing to lose.

— Robin Williams

The Falklands thing was a fight between two bald men over a comb.

— Jorge Luis Borges

It is easier to fight for one's principles than to live up to them.

— Alfred Adler

Always walk away from a fight. Then ambush.

— Tim Dorsey

It's empowering knowing that I can break a man's nose with my elbow.

— Gwendoline Christie

I do not believe in using women in combat, because females are too fierce.

— Margaret Mead

If everyone who had a gun just shot themselves, there wouldn't be a problem.

— George Harrison

If you talk bad about country music, it's like saying bad things about my momma. Them's fightin' words.

— Dolly Parton

My toughest fight was with my first wife.

— **Muhammad Ali**

God created war so that Americans would learn geography.

— **Mark Twain**

It is forbidden to kill; therefore all murderers are punished unless they kill in large numbers and to the sound of trumpets.

— **Voltaire**

I had a romance novel inside me, but I paid three sailors to beat it out of me with steel pipes.

— **Patton Oswalt**

If violence wasn't your last resort, you failed to resort to enough of it.

— **Howard Tayler**

Football combines the two worst features of American life. It's violence punctuated by committee meetings.

— **George F. Will**

We don't just borrow words; on occasion, English has pursued other languages down alleyways to beat them unconscious and rifle their pockets for new vocabulary.

— **James Nicoll**

A gun is a necessity. Who knows if you're walking down a street and you spot a moose?

— **Pat Paulsen**

A soft answer turneth away wrath. Once wrath is looking the other way, shoot it in the head.

— **Howard Tayler**

JESUS H. CHRIST!

God save us from people who mean well.

— **Vikram Seth**

If we are all God's children, what's so special about Jesus?

— **Jimmy Carr**

How much reverence can you have for a Supreme Being who finds it necessary to include such phenomena as phlegm and tooth decay in His divine system of creation?

— **Joseph Heller**

You wonder if God doesn't have an answering machine to screen out the prayers of the venal and the boring? And in which category has he placed you?

— **Tom Robbins**

Anyone who thinks sitting in church can make you a Christian must also think that sitting in a garage can make you a car.

— **Garrison Keillor**

Alcohol may be man's worst enemy, but the bible says love your enemy.

— **Frank Sinatra**

The invisible and the non-existent look very much alike.

— **Delos B. McKown**

When one person suffers from a delusion, it is called insanity. When many people suffer from a delusion it is called a religion.

— **Robert M. Pirsig**

If Jesus came back and saw what was being done in his name, he'd never stop throwing up.

— **Woody Allen**

Be sure to lie to your kids about the benevolent, all-seeing Santa Claus. It will prepare them for an adulthood of believing in God.

— **Scott Dikkers**

I would never want to be a member of a group whose symbol was a man nailed to two pieces of wood.

— George Carlin

Hearing nuns' confessions is like being stoned to death with popcorn.

— Fulton J. Sheen

I want Jesus to come back and say, "That's not what I meant!"

— Margaret Cho

Yes, reason has been a part of organized religion, ever since two nudists took dietary advice from a talking snake.

— Jon Stewart

Forgive, O Lord, my little jokes on Thee / And I'll forgive Thy great big one on me.

— Robert Frost

In heaven, all the interesting people are missing.

— **Friedrich Nietzsche**

Look for God like a man with his head on fire looks for water.

— **Elizabeth Gilbert**

Properly read, the Bible is the most potent force for atheism ever conceived.

— **Isaac Asimov**

If you think God's there, He is. If you don't, He isn't. And if that's what God's like, I wouldn't worry about it.

— **Haruki Murakami**

The real question of life after death isn't whether or not it exists, but even if it does what problem this really solves.

— **Ludwig Wittgenstein**

Religion is what keeps the poor from murdering the rich.

— **Napoleon Bonaparte**

If there is a God, atheism must seem to Him as less of an insult than religion.

— **Edmond de Goncourt**

Men will never be free until the last king is strangled with the entrails of the last priest.

— **Denis Diderot**

You won't burn in hell. But be nice anyway.

— **Ricky Gervais**

ELECTED OFFICE

When I was a boy I was told that anybody could become president; I'm beginning to believe it.

— Clarence Darrow

A lot has been said about politics; some of it complimentary, but most of it accurate.

— Eric Idle

Politics is such a torment that I advise everyone I love not to mix with it.

— Thomas Jefferson

Politics is not the art of the possible. It consists in choosing between the disastrous and the unpalatable.

— John Kenneth Galbraith

We'd all like t'vote fer th'best man, but he's never a candidate.

— Kin Hubbard

The truth will set you free but first it will piss you off.

— Gloria Steinem

Instead of giving a politician the keys to the city, it might be better to change the locks.

— Doug Larson

A politician needs the ability to foretell what is going to happen tomorrow, next week, next month, and next year. And to have the ability afterwards to explain why it didn't happen.

— Winston Churchill

Being president is like being a jackass in a hailstorm. There's nothing to do but to stand there and take it.

— Lyndon B. Johnson

Good thing we've still got politics in Texas—finest form of free entertainment ever invented.

— Molly Ivins

In modern American politics, being the right kind of ignorant and entertainingly crazy is like having a big right hand in boxing; you've always got a puncher's chance.

— **Matt Taibbi**

Now I know what a statesman is; he's a dead politician. We need more statesmen.

— **Bob Edwards**

Illegal aliens have always been a problem in the United States. Ask any Indian.

— **Robert Orben**

The whole aim of practical politics is to keep the populace alarmed (and hence clamorous to be led to safety) by menacing it with an endless series of hobgoblins, all of them imaginary.

— **H. L. Mencken**

Too bad that all the people who know how to run
the country are busy driving taxicabs and cutting hair.

— **George Burns**

A fool and his money are soon elected.

— **Will Rogers**

VOTE, n. The instrument and symbol of a freeman's
power to make a fool of himself and a wreck of his
country.

— **Ambrose Bierce**

An appeaser is one who feeds a crocodile, hoping it will
eat him last.

— **Winston Churchill**

Patriotism is, fundamentally, a conviction that a
particular country is the best in the world because
you were born in it.

— **George Bernard Shaw**

Half of the American people have never read a newspaper.
Half never voted for president. One hopes it is the
same half.

— **Gore Vidal**

Anyone who is capable of getting themselves made
president should on no account be allowed to do
the job.

— **Douglas Adams**

THE FOURTH ESTATE

A journalist is a machine that converts coffee into copy.

— **Michael Ryan Elgan**

I don't so much mind that newspapers are dying—it's watching them commit suicide that pisses me off.

— **Molly Ivins**

Freedom of the press is limited to those who own one.

— **A. J. Liebling**

Myth is much more important and true than history. History is just journalism ... and you know how reliable that is.

— **Joseph Campbell**

Journalism consists largely in saying "Lord James is dead" to people who never knew Lord James was alive.

— **G. K. Chesterton**

Better a good journalist than a poor assassin.

— **Jean-Paul Sartre**

I became a journalist because I did not want to rely on newspapers for information.

— **Christopher Hitchens**

If one morning I walked on top of the water across the Potomac River, the headline that afternoon would read: "President Can't Swim."

— **Lyndon B. Johnson**

Accuracy to a newspaper is what virtue is to a lady; but a newspaper can always print a retraction.

— **Adlai Stevenson**

If I want to knock a story off the front page, I just change my hairstyle.

— **Hillary Rodham Clinton**

Let's be honest about journalists: We find a lot of ways of being wrong.

— E. J. Dionne Jr.

Journalism will kill you, but it will keep you alive while you're at it.

— Horace Greeley

Objective journalism and an opinion column are about as similar as the Bible and *Playboy* magazine.

— Walter Cronkite

Laziness has become the chief characteristic of journalism, displacing incompetence.

— Kingsley Amis

Most rock journalism is people who can't write, interviewing people who can't talk, for people who can't read.

— Frank Zappa

Journalism—an ability to meet the challenge of filling the space.

— Rebecca West

I think I prefer books to people—primary sources scare me.

— Tom Rachman

The media has changed. We now give broadcast licenses to philosophies instead of people.

— Gary Ackerman

One reason that cats are happier than people is that they have no newspapers.

— Gwendolyn Brooks

The man who reads nothing at all is better educated than the man who reads nothing but newspapers.

— Thomas Jefferson

The evening papers print what they do and get away with it because by afternoon the human mind is ruined anyhow.

— **Christopher Morley**

Journalism is organized gossip.

— **Edward Egglestone**

The one function TV news performs very well is that when there is no news we give it to you with the same emphasis as if there were.

— **David Brinkley**

Being a reporter is as much a diagnosis as a job description.

— **Anna Quindlen**

News is something someone wants suppressed. Everything else is just advertising.

— **Lord Northcliff**

Freedom of the press in Britain is freedom to print such
of the proprietor's prejudices as the advertisers won't
object to.

— **Hannen Swaffer**

Sacrificing good men to journalism is like sending
William Faulkner to work for *Time* magazine.

— **Hunter S. Thompson**

Trying to determine what is going on in the world by
reading newspapers is like trying to tell the time by
watching the second hand of a clock.

— **Ben Hecht**

THE BOOB
TUBE

It seems to me that television is exactly like a gun. Your enjoyment of it is determined by which end of it you're on.

— **Alfred Hitchcock**

If we were to do the "Second Coming of Christ" in color for a full hour, there would be a considerable number of stations which would decline to carry it on the grounds that a Western or a quiz show would be more profitable.

— **Edward R. Murrow**

I find television very educating. Every time somebody turns on the set, I go into the other room and read a book.

— **Groucho Marx**

Television is an invention that permits you to be entertained in your living room by people you wouldn't have in your home.

— **David Frost**

Watching television is like taking black spray paint to your third eye.

— **Bill Hicks**

Modern broadcast television, with its digital boxes
and fiber optics and orbiting geosynchronous satellites,
has become a perfectly engineered slaughterhouse
of time.

— **Daniel R. Thorne**

In day-to-day commerce, television is not so much
interested in the business of communications as in the
business of delivering audiences to advertisers. People
are the merchandise, not the shows. The shows are
merely the bait.

— **Les Brown**

Television characters live inside our minds as though
they're actual people. In fact, we know more about
them than we do about most people in our physical lives.

— **Neal Pollack**

I won't say that all senior citizens who can't master technology should be publicly flogged, but if we made an example of one or two, it might give the others incentive to try harder.

— **Chuck Lorre**

Imitation is the sincerest form of television.

— **Fred Allen**

Never pass up a chance to have sex or appear on television.

— **Gore Vidal**

All [television] shows are like cigarettes. You watch two, you have a higher chance of watching three. They're all addictive.

— **Dan Harmon**

Seeing a murder on television ... can help work off one's antagonisms. And if you haven't any antagonisms, the commercials will give you some.

— **Alfred Hitchcock**

On my tombstone, I want written, "He never did *Love Boat*!"

— Orson Welles

Television is democracy at its ugliest.

— Paddy Chayefsky

In Beverly Hills ... they don't throw their garbage away. They make it into television shows.

— Woody Allen

Television is chewing gum for the eyes.

— Frank Lloyd Wright

Television is just one more facet of that considerable segment of our society that never had any standard but the soft buck.

— Raymond Chandler

Every time you think television has hit its lowest ebb,
a new program comes along to make you wonder where
you thought the ebb was.

— **Art Buchwald**

Hey, if I had my choice for social engineering, I'd
declare an automatic R-rating for any movie that
depicts television commercials.

— **Marshall Herskovitz**

I never weigh myself, but the brutal truth of television
is that they don't employ old people or fat people.

— **Ruby Wax**

I don't watch television. It destroys the art of talking
about oneself.

— **Stephen Fry**

FOOLS

The problem with the world is that everyone does not have a brain, but everyone does have a tongue.

— **Raheel Farooq**

Men are born ignorant, not stupid. They are made stupid by education.

— **Bertrand Russell**

She doesn't understand the concept of Roman numerals. She thought we just fought in World War Eleven.

— **Joan Rivers**

Two things are infinite: the universe and human stupidity; and I'm not sure about the universe.

— **Albert Einstein**

I am not the sharpest knife in the knife-thing.

— **Jimmy Dore**

In politics, stupidity is not a handicap.

— **Napoleon Bonaparte**

Let us be thankful for the fools. But for them the rest of us could not succeed.

— **Mark Twain**

I am fairly certain that "YOLO" is just "Carpe Diem" for stupid people.

— **Jack Black**

Sometimes I wonder whether the world is being run by smart people who are putting us on or by imbeciles who really mean it.

— **Laurence J. Peter**

There are some remarks that are so stupid that to be even vaguely aware of them is the intellectual equivalent of living next door to Chernobyl.

— **Elizabeth Wurtzel**

A stupid man's report of what a clever man says can never be accurate, because he unconsciously translates what he hears into something he can understand.

— **Bertrand Russell**

Nobody ever did anything very foolish except from some strong principle.

— **Lord Melbourne**

Human beings can always be relied upon to exert, with vigor, their God-given right to be stupid.

— **Dean Koontz**

I'm all in favor of the democratic principle that one idiot is as good as one genius, but I draw the line when someone takes the next step and concludes that two idiots are better than one genius.

— **Leo Szilard**

Seriousness is stupidity sent to college.

— **P. J. O'Rourke**

One person is never as stupid as a group of people. That's why they have lynch mobs, not lynch individuals.

— **Ben Horowitz**

Hundreds of wise men cannot make the world a heaven, but one idiot is enough to turn it into a hell.

— **Raheel Farooq**

Never argue with an idiot. They will drag you down to their level and beat you with experience.

— **Sarah Cook**

The kind of man who wants the government to adopt and enforce his ideas is always the kind of man whose ideas are idiotic.

— **H. L. Mencken**

Nothing is more humiliating than to see idiots succeed in enterprises we have failed in.

— **Gustave Flaubert**

Stupidity combined with arrogance and a huge ego will get you a long way.

— **Chris Lowe**

Against stupidity the gods themselves contend in vain.

— **Friedrich von Schiller**

One should commit no stupidity twice, the variety of choice is, in the end, large enough.

— **Jean-Paul Sartre**

If you're feeling cocky, it's because there's something you don't know.

— **Eoin Colfer**

THE INFORMATION
SUPERHIGHWAY

Oh, Wikipedia, with your tension between those who would share knowledge and those who would destroy it.

— **John Green**

I have one major problem with the Internet: It's full of liars.

— **John Lydon**

Dear Internet: You are very good at spreading rumors. Truth is more valuable and much harder to come by.

— **Mark Frost**

[I]t's been my policy to view the Internet not as an "information highway," but as an electronic asylum filled with babbling loonies.

— **Mike Royko**

I swear on everything holy I do not know what's on the Internet about me.

— **Iris Apfel**

I am regularly asked what the average Internet user can do to ensure his security. My first answer is usually "Nothing; you're screwed."

— Bruce Schneier

I find it interesting that there are impostors out on the Internet pretending to be Werner Herzog.

— Werner Herzog

The Internet is a bastion of negativity, and we get to sit there and voice our cute, little, important opinions.

— Roger Craig Smith

The Internet is just a world passing around notes in a classroom.

— Jon Stewart

The day I made that statement [about the inventing the internet], I was tired because I'd been up all night inventing the Camcorder.

— Al Gore

Can we go back to using Facebook for what it was originally for—looking up exes to see how fat they got?

— **Bill Maher**

There is a lot of talk in publishing these days that we need to become more like the Internet: We need to make books for short attention spans with bells and whistles—books, in short, that are as much like "Angry Birds" as possible.

— **John Green**

Cars will soon have the Internet on the dashboard. I worry that this will distract me from my texting.

— **Andy Borowitz**

Toyota has announced it will start integrating Microsoft technology into their vehicles. It's perfect for the person who wants a car that crashes every ten minutes.

— **Conan O'Brien**

Bill Gates is a very rich man today ... and do you want to know why? The answer is one word: versions.

— **Dave Barry**

The digital camera is a great invention because it allows us to reminisce. Instantly.

— **Demetri Martin**

Technology has really changed parenting. There's a whole generation of kids whose only childhood memory of their dad will be his bald spot bent over a Blackberry.

— **Kate Deimling**

My life is now a constant assessment of whether what's happening in real life is more entertaining than what's happening on my phone.

— **Damien Fahey**

The real problem is not whether machines think but whether men do.

— **B. F. Skinner**

My computer could be more encouraging. You know, instead of "invalid password," why not something like, "Ooooh, you're so close!"?

— Lisa Porter

Give a man a fish, and he will eat for a day. Give a man Twitter, and he will forget to eat and starve to death.

— Andy Borowitz

OUR LEGAL SYSTEM

Lawyers, I suppose, were children once.

— **Charles Lamb**

Animals have these advantages over man: They have no theologians to instruct them, their funerals cost them nothing, and no one starts lawsuits over their wills.

— **Voltaire**

You can't learn everything you need to know legally.

— **John Irving**

Only one thing is impossible for God: To find any sense in any copyright law on the planet.

— **Mark Twain**

I busted a mirror and got seven years bad luck, but my lawyer thinks he can get me five.

— **Steven Wright**

Make crime pay. Become a lawyer.

— **Will Rogers**

Laws are spider webs through which the big flies pass and the little ones get caught.

— **Honoré de Balzac**

I wonder how much the general population of this country know that the legal system has far more to do with playing a good hand of poker than it does with justice.

— **Jodi Picoult**

Lawyers are the only persons in whom ignorance of the law is not punished.

— **Jeremy Bentham**

Unfortunately, what many people forget is that judges are just lawyers in robes.

— **Tammy Bruce**

I've always thought legal addictions are a great way to create a business. Starbucks is a wonderful example.

— **Nolan Bushnell**

A lawyer is a learned gentleman who rescues your estate from your enemies and keeps it to himself.

— **Henry Bougham**

The best way to get a bad law repealed is to enforce it strictly.

— **Abraham Lincoln**

An incompetent lawyer can delay a trial for months or years. A competent lawyer can delay one even longer.

— **Evelle Younger**

Where there's a will, there's a lawsuit.

— **Addison Mizner**

I believe ... that while all human life is sacred
there's nothing wrong with the death penalty if you
can trust the legal system implicitly, and that no one
but a moron would ever trust the legal system.

— **Neil Gaiman**

Lawyers spend a great deal of their time shoveling
smoke.

— **Oliver Wendell Holmes Jr.**

A lawyer with a briefcase can steal more than a thousand
men with guns.

— **Mario Puzo**

A lawyer will do anything to win a case, sometimes he
will even tell the truth.

— **Patrick Murray**

The one great principle of English law is to make business
for itself.

— **Charles Dickens**

If Moses had gone to Harvard Law School and spent three years working on the Hill, he would have written the Ten Commandments with three exceptions and a saving clause.

— **Charles Morgan**

Lawyers are men whom we hire to protect us from lawyers.

— **Elbert Hubbard**

Only lawyers and mental defectives are automatically exempt for jury duty.

— **George Bernard Shaw**

The only way you can beat the lawyers is to die with nothing.

— **Will Rogers**

Lawyers should never marry other lawyers. This is called "inbreeding," from which comes idiot children and more lawyers.

— **Kip Lurie**

LITIGATION, n. A machine which you go into as a pig and come out of as a sausage.

— **Ambrose Bierce**

Injustice is easy to bear, what stings is justice.

— **H. L. Mencken**

SHOWBIZ

[*Armageddon*] is an assault on the eyes, the ears, the brain, common sense, and the human desire to be entertained. No matter what they're charging to get in, it's worth more to get out.

— **Roger Ebert**

Hollywood's all about getting really creative people and then just putting the thumbscrews to them until they cry.

— **James Cameron**

People never forget two things, their first love and the money they wasted watching a bad movie.

— **Amit Kalantri**

Never judge a book by its movie.

— **J. W. Eagan**

In this business, until you're known as a monster, you're not a star.

— **Bette Davis**

The length of a film should be directly related to the endurance of the human bladder.

— **Alfred Hitchcock**

I'm a Hollywood writer, so I put on my sports jacket and take off my brain.

— **Ben Hecht**

Academia is the death of cinema. It is the very opposite of passion. Film is not the art of scholars, but of illiterates.

— **Werner Herzog**

Movies are so rarely great art that if we cannot appreciate great trash we have very little reason to be interested in them.

— **Pauline Kael**

You can take all the sincerity in Hollywood, place it in the navel of a fruit fly, and still have room enough for three caraway seeds and a producer's heart.

— **Fred Allen**

I believe that God felt sorry for actors so he created Hollywood to give them a place in the sun and a swimming pool. The price they had to pay was to surrender their talent.

— **Cedric Hardwicke**

In Hollywood the woods are full of people that learned to write but evidently can't read. If they could read their stuff, they'd stop writing.

— **Will Rogers**

[Hollywood's] ... vision of the rewarding movie is a vehicle for ... some male idol of the muddled millions with a permanent hangover, six worn-out acting tricks, the build of a lifeguard, and the mentality of a chicken-strangler.

— **Raymond Chandler**

In Hollywood, the real stars are all in animation. Alvin and the Chipmunks don't throw star fits, don't demand custom-designed Winnebagos, and are a breeze at costume fittings.

— **John Waters**

The only reason I'm in Hollywood is that I don't have the moral courage to refuse the money.

— **Marlon Brando**

My folks came to U.S. as immigrants, aliens, and became citizens. I was born in Boston, a citizen, went to Hollywood and became an alien.

— **Leonard Nimoy**

Hollywood is a place where they place you under contract instead of under observation.

— **Walter Winchell**

I always thought the real violence in Hollywood isn't what's on the screen. It's what you have to do to raise the money.

— **David Mamet**

Hollywood is wonderful. Anyone who doesn't like it is either crazy or sober.

— **Raymond Chandler**

What's so wonderful about football and business and show business is that every time I start thinking I'm special, I get knocked on my ass.

— **Fran Tarkenton**

There's nothing the matter with Hollywood that a good earthquake couldn't cure.

— **Moss Hart**

Nihilism is best done by professionals.

— **Iggy Pop**

THIS IS THE END

I am ready to meet my Maker. Whether my Maker is pre-pared for the great ordeal of meeting me is another matter.

— **Winston Churchill**

The art of dying graciously is nowhere advertised, in spite of the fact that its market potential is great.

— **Milton Mayer**

It's not that I'm afraid to die, I just don't want to be there when it happens.

— **Woody Allen**

Death is just nature's way of telling you to slow down.

— **Dick Sharples**

According to most studies, people's number one fear is public speaking. Number two is death. Death is number two! Does that sound right? This means to the average person, if you go to a funeral, you're better off in the casket than doing the eulogy.

— **Jerry Seinfeld**

I never wanted to see anybody die, but there are a few obituary notices I have read with pleasure.

— Clarence Darrow

Afraid of death? Not at all. Be a great relief. Then I wouldn't have to talk to you.

— Katharine Hepburn

Death is not the end. There remains the litigation over the estate.

— Ambrose Bierce

Men should think twice before making widowhood women's only path to power.

— Gloria Steinem

Life does not cease to be funny when people die any more than it ceases to be serious when people laugh.

— George Bernard Shaw

Suicide is man's way of telling God, "You can't fire me—
I quit."

— **Bill Maher**

Dying is a very dull, dreary affair. And my advice to you
is to have nothing whatever to do with it.

— **W. Somerset Maugham**

Die? I should say not, dear fellow. No Barrymore would
allow such a conventional thing to happen to him.

— **John Barrymore**

My uncle Sammy was an angry man. He had printed on
his tombstone: What are you looking at?

— **Margaret Smith**

If you don't know how to die, don't worry; Nature will tell
you what to do on the spot, fully and adequately.

— **Montaigne**

If you live each day as it was your last, someday you'll most certainly be right.

— Steve Jobs

The meaning of life is that it stops.

— Franz Kafka

Most people die at twenty-five and aren't buried until they're seventy-five.

— Benjamin Franklin

I want to die like my father, peacefully in his sleep, not screaming and terrified, like his passengers.

— Bob Monkhouse

My wallpaper and I are fighting a duel to the death. One or the other of us has to go.

— Oscar Wilde,
on his deathbed

Any man who has $10,000 left when he dies is a failure.

— **Errol Flynn**

Death is the last enemy: once we've got past that I think everything will be alright.

— **Alice Thomas Ellis**

What's the difference between life and a *Saturday Night Live* sketch? Life doesn't go on forever.

— **Eric Idle**

I want it reported that I drowned in moonlight, strangled by my own bra.

— **Carrie Fisher,**
on how she wanted her obituary to read